D1232832

FAITH AND THE FUTURE

JOSEPH CARDINAL RATZINGER
(POPE BENEDICT XVI)

Faith and the Future

IGNATIUS PRESS   SAN FRANCISCO

Original German edition:
Glaube und Zukunft
by Joseph Ratzinger/Benedict XVI
© 1970 by Kösel-Verlag, Division of Verlagsgruppe
Random House GmbH, München, Germany

Original English edition published by
Franciscan Herald Press
© 1971 by Franciscan Herald Press
Published with ecclesiastical approval, 1971
Reprinted by permission of the
Center for Faith Development & Spirituality
at Quincy University

Salvator Mundi, c. 1550 (tempera on panel),
Alessandro Allori (1535–1607) /
Pinacoteca Ambrosiana, Milan, Italy /
© Veneranda Biblioteca Ambrosiana /
Paolo Manusardi/Mondadori Portfolio /
Bridgeman Images

Cover design by John Herreid

Published by Ignatius Press, San Francisco, 2009
Paperback edition published 2019
ISBN 978-1-62164-323-4
Library of Congress Control Number 2008934739
Printed in the United States of America ∞

For Professor Johann Baptist Auer
on his sixtieth birthday

About This Book

Increasingly, the future is becoming a theme for theological reflection. In the background we can detect a growing concern for the future of faith. Does faith have any future at all, and, if so, where in all the confusion of today's trends will we discover its embryo? But the problem of the future assails not only the believer. In the ever more rapidly advancing process of historical evolution man is confronted with enormous opportunities, but also with colossal perils. For him, the future is not only hope, but sorrow—a nightmare, indeed. He cannot avoid asking what part faith can play in building tomorrow's world. The author approaches this problem from a variety of angles, and finishes off with a sketch of the future of the Church.

Contents

Preface

The five chapters of this book were first presented as radio addresses. The first three were
broadcast in the special program of the Bavarian
Rundfunk during December 1969, the fourth on
Vatican Radio in February 1970, and the fifth by
the Hessian Rundfunk at Christmas 1969. As it
happened, all five addresses centered round the
same theme: the problem of faith and the future. The fact that this problem emerges on every side today indicates how faith is being shaken
to its foundation by the crisis of the present and
also how great is the fascination of the future
in a period when we witness history being set
unusually in motion and see human possibilities
beginning to develop, positively and negatively,
along roads that lead we know not where. And
so, the reflections in this little book cannot be
considered as "final". They are presented merely
as attempts at "opening up", at indicating where

the embryonic future is to be detected—and that is within faith, provided faith remains true to itself.

Joseph Ratzinger
Regensburg
Spring 1970

Faith and Knowledge

Over a hundred years ago the French philosopher and sociologist Auguste Comte distinguished three phases in the historical evolution of human thought: the theological-fictive; the metaphysical-abstract; the positive. Gradually the positivist form of thinking would come to be applied to all departments of reality. Finally even the most complicated and least comprehensible department, the ultimate, longest defended citadel of theology, would be successfully subjected to positivist scientific analysis and exposition. Moral phenomena and man himself—his essential human nature—would become subject matter for the positive sciences. Here, too, the mystery of the theologians would little by little have to lose ground to the advance of positivist thinking. In the end, it would be possible to develop even a "social physics", no less exact than the physics that charts the inanimate world. In the process, the realm of the priest would ultimately vanish, and questions about the nature of reality would be handed over totally to the competence of scholars. In the wake of this development, the question about God's existence would of necessity become obsolete, discarded and left behind by man's mind as quite simply meaningless. Just as today it never occurs to anyone to deny the existence of the Homeric gods, because the question about their existence is not even taken seriously, so when thinking had finally assumed the positivist form, the question about the existence of God of itself ceased to exist. For this reason Comte was spared the excitement of a war against God, such as other great atheists before and after his day have waged with the utmost passion. Comte simply strode calmly on toward the post-theistic age. Moreover, in his late period he applied himself at great length to the task of drafting a new religion for mankind, for although, as he affirmed, man can live without God, he cannot live without religion.[1]

It seems incontrovertible that today the mentality described by Comte is that of a very large

---

[1] On Comte, cf. H. de Lubac, *The Drama of Atheist Humanism*, trans. Edith M. Riley, Anne Englund Nash, and Mark Sebanc (San Francisco: Ignatius Press, 1995), pp. 131–267.

section of human society. The question about
God no longer finds any place in human thought.
To take up a well-known saying of Laplace, the
context of the world is self-contained, and the
hypothesis of God is no longer necessary for its
comprehension. Even the faithful, like travelers
on a sinking ship, are becoming widely affected
by an uneasy feeling: they are asking if the Christian faith has any future, or if it is not, in fact,
more and more obviously being made obsolete
by intellectual evolution. Behind such notions
is the sense that a great gulf is developing between the world of faith and the world of science, a gulf that seems unbridgeable, so that faith
is made very largely impracticable.

Let us take a look at the general picture and
see where the critical points are to be found.
The difficulty begins with the very first page
of the Bible. The concept presented there of
how the world came to be is in direct contradiction of all that we know today about the ori-
gins of the universe; and even if the word has got
around that these passages in the Bible are not
meant to be a textbook of natural science and so
need not be taken as a literal description of how
the universe came to be, still, an uneasy feeling

remains: the fear that this explanation is a retrospective evasion, unsupported by the original texts themselves. And the problem continues, almost page by page, as we read on through the Bible. There is the clay, molded into a man by the hand of God, and then, close upon it, the picture of woman formed out of the side of the sleeping man, flesh of his flesh and companion to comfort his loneliness. Today we may be learning how to reappraise this imagery as a profoundly symbolic utterance about human nature, as pictures whose truth lies on a plane totally different from that upon which biology and the theory of descent operate. We may now see these pictures as indeed expressing truth, but a truth that is deeper and more concerned with man's essential humanity than are the truths of natural science, exact and important as the latter may be. This may well be, but in the very next chapter new problems emerge with the story of the Fall. How can one bring this into harmony with the knowledge that, on the evidence of natural science, man starts, not from above, but from below, does not fall, but slowly rises, even now having only just accomplished the metamorphosis from animal to human being? And what of paradise? Long before man existed, pain and death were in the world. Thistles and thorns grew long before any man had set eyes on them. And another thing: the first man was scarcely self-conscious, knew only privation and the wearisome struggle to survive. He was far from possessing the full endowment of reason, which the old doctrine of paradise attributes to him. But once the picture of paradise and the Fall has been broken in pieces, the notion of original sin goes with it, to be followed logically, it would seem, by the notion of redemption as well.

Obviously, we might here employ arguments similar to those we have already used concerning the divine potter who infused spirit into the clay of the earth to create man. Here, too, I say, we make it apparent that the truth about man goes deeper than the conclusions of biology. From the biological point of view, man starts off from below; but it is still not by any means clear whether man really starts from below or whether perhaps his true beginning, the point of departure of the essence of humanity, is not above—to speak in pictures, the symbolism of which is still meaningful for us, even if our universe has long since ceased to acknowledge fixed points of reference,

"above", "below", "right", and "left" having become interchangeable according to the stand-
point of the calculating observer. But it is always difficult to apply such arguments as these:
the operation belongs beyond the horizon of our
normal thinking, which tends rather to come up
at this point with a firm refutation.

Let us continue, therefore, to assess the problems and contradictions that oppress the common mind, in order to measure to the utmost all
the severity of the problem that emerges under
the title "Faith and Knowledge". After the Fall,
the problem continues with the biblical picture of
history, which goes on at once to portray Adam
as living in a cultural phase dated about 4,000
B.C. This date does in fact agree with the biblical
chronology, which allows some four thousand
years from creation until Christ. Today every-
body knows, however, that before this phase was
reached, hundreds of thousands of years of human life and effort had already run their course,
and these find no place in the biblical historical
picture, which is set strictly within the framework of ancient Eastern thought.

This brings us to the next problem: the Bible,
venerated by faith as the word of God, has been

disclosed to us, by historical-critical scholarship, as a thoroughly human book. Not only are its literary forms those of the world that produced it, but its manner of thought, even in respect of genuinely religious topics, has been determined by the world in which it arose. Are we still able to believe in the God who called out to Moses from the burning bush, who smote the first-born of Egypt, who led his people in war against the Canaanites, who struck down Uzzah dead because he dared to put out his hand to steady the Ark of the Covenant? For us, is all of this not just the ancient East—interesting and significant, perhaps, as a phase in human consciousness, but only a phase in human consciousness, not the expression of divine utterance? One can recall, it is true, how Pascal, one of the great minds in the evolution of the natural sciences, sewed into the lining of his coat a piece of paper bearing these words: "The God of Abraham, of Isaac, and of Jacob, not of the philosophers". His experience had been precisely of an anthropomorphic God, of a God who was close to man, of a God who spoke and acted and loved and was angry. It was only in such a God that he had at last discovered the authentic divinity of God in contrast to the artifacts of human speculation; but how long he suffered before he saw the fire of the burning bush shining through all the curiosities of the Old Testament and heard the voice of the living God! Which of us has the strength or the patience to endure such suffering and find such an experience, so often contradicted by appearance? For all the miraculous stories of the Old Testament are still there, not so much a sign of faith for us today as an obstacle to it, and the expression of a cosmology that regards the universe as ruled by all manner of spirits, not in accordance with fixed laws, but by caprice, so that miracles seem every bit as normal as they are alien in a world ruled by rational principles.

Let us now pass to the New Testament. There can be no doubt that it moves us much more deeply than the Old. The spirit that pervades it still appeals to us immediately, in contrast to the frequently grisly and uncanny stories contained in not a few of the Old Testament texts. But, in the last analysis, the demand it makes upon us is even greater. All of history now becomes linked up to the person of Jesus of Nazareth. A single man is supposed to be the center of all history, the watershed of human destiny. Is this not the naive claim of an age that was simply incapable of penetrating the vastness of the universe, the greatness of history and of the world? Is Indian philosophy not nearer the mark when it speaks of a multiplicity of Avatars of God, of divine descents, in each of which a new fragment of the eternal is revealed or in each of which the eternal reveals itself to the temporal; but in such a way that none of these is God himself in his unsurpassable and necessary form? Indian philosophers do not hesitate to recognize Jesus of Nazareth as an Avatar of God, just like Krishna, Buddha, and many others. These are all divine *epiphanies*, reflections in time of the eternal. In every one of these something of God is made visible; they all bring God close to man; but none of them *is* God. They are like the color of the rainbow: refractions of one light, none excluding any other, all interdependent.[2] How pious that all sounds, and how intelligible when compared with the claim of the Christian faith: Jesus is God, true man and

---

[2] Cf. J. Neuner, "Das Christusmysterium und die indische Lehre von den Avatāras", in *Das Konzil von Chalkedon*, ed. A. Grillmeier and H. Bacht, 3:785–824 (Wurzburg, 1954); C. Regamey, "Die Religionen Indiens", in *Christus und die Religionen der Erde*, ed. F. König, 2nd ed., 3:73–227, esp. 157–62 (Vienna, 1956).

true God, not just an epiphany, but the substance
of the eternal, through whom God binds himself radically and irrevocably to the world. I am
firmly convinced that the dispute so much in
vogue today about the virgin birth is merely an
evasion of the real problem, for a God who is
able to become man can also be born of a virgin,
thereby providing a sign of his uniqueness. But
can God be man? A man, completely human and
at the same time true God and, hence, entitled
to demand faith from all and in all ages?

Or is this not simply a case of putting too high
a value on a moment from the past? Once again,
are we not encountering a view of the universe
that we no longer share: the earth as the floor
of the universe, with the arch of heaven above,
so that the earth is indeed the lowest and the
most insignificant part and, yet, the foundation
of everything, thus the most reasonable site for
the encounter between the Creator and his creation? Even if one is prepared to accept in principle the notion of the incarnation of God, the
claim made by the Christian faith still has a question to face: Why did God not bear plainer tes-
timony to himself? Why did he not make himself perceptible to all, so that every man might

clearly recognize him and be able to say: "There is God"?

The list of difficulties that seem to make faith and knowledge irreconcilable continues as soon as we cross the threshold of the New Testament and step onto the road of Church history. First comes the question: Where precisely is the Church? Which of the contesting parties ought one to support? Were there from the very start merely conflicting confessions, so that men have always been offered no more than the choice of some partial Christianity or been set the task of seeking Christianity behind or in spite of the Churches? At all events, the claim of the several Churches seems to be called in question by their mutual conflict, which diminishes their reliability and credibility. And then the problems we have already indicated are continued in the problems of the Church's teaching. Does the dogma of the Trinity really express the faith of the Bible, or is it not rather the product of the Greek mind, which thus gratifies its thirst for speculation? Whatever the answer to that question, we still have to ask: What exactly does it mean when we say that God is three-in-one? Does this affirm a reality that means anything to us today? Jumping over all the other affirmations of the patristic age that present obstacles to us today, let us take but a single example from medieval dogma, one that recently has aroused much interest: the doctrine of transubstantiation, of the essential change of the eucharistic offerings. As it is, the subtle meaning of this definition can be represented by the ordinary intellect only in a rough manner, so that what is indicated is bound to seem forever unattainable, especially as there is the additional difficulty that the medieval concept of substance has long since become inaccessible to us. Insofar as we use the concept of substance at all today, we understand thereby the ultimate particles of matter, and the chemically complex mixture that is bread certainly does not fall into that category. And even if reflection is able patiently to clarify many things here, the question remains: Why must it all be so complicated? Does the very fact that this can be grasped only through a multiplicity of complicated interpretations not suggest that here we have something obsolete and possessing no present power?

And this, so it seems to me, is where we finally come up against the real uneasiness that we men of today feel when we consider the juxtaposition of faith and knowledge; and it is also the point at which we may attempt to feel around for an answer. The thing about the Christian faith that really troubles us is to a large extent the burden of the plethora of definitions, which have accumulated in the course of history and which now present themselves to men, all demanding the assent of faith. That our immediate difficulty lies here can be seen from the extraordinary sympathetic resonance that is aroused when an author seems to penetrate the multiplicity of definitions and resolve them all in the unity of a simple assent of faith. Over and over again we hear how this book or that lecture has produced a liberating effect; and this shows plainly that men today feel the form of faith as a burden and yet at the same time are inspired by the desire to believe, otherwise they would find it quite easy simply to drop the whole thing without more ado. And so, any liberation by theologians that gives people the feeling that they still remain within the fabric of the faith is not questioned. Paradoxical as it may seem, the days in which we live are very much characterized by a yearning for faith: the world of planned economy, of research, of exact calculation and experiment is quite obviously not enough to satisfy people. Fundamentally, people want to be liberated from this just as much as from the old-fashioned faith that, by its contradiction of modern knowledge, has become such an oppressive burden to them. But it could not be a burden if we did not feel ourselves somehow affected or moved by it, if there were not something here that calls us to search farther.

We will have to reflect a little longer on this curious situation in which the man of today finds himself before we attempt to define the real meaning of faith, for our life today is marked not only by dissatisfaction with faith, but equally by dissatisfaction with the world of science. Only if we describe this *double* dissatisfaction—not foreseen by Auguste Comte—will we provide a reasonably fair representation of the presuppositions of the problem of faith and knowledge today. The curious thing about the time in which we live is this: the moment in which modern thought becomes self-sufficient is the very moment in which its dissatisfaction becomes most apparent, and it inevitably falls prey to relativism. We will have to consider this point in more detail in the third chapter; meantime, however, a brief mention will suffice. Positivism, which emerged at first as a demand for a particular method to be adopted within the exact sciences, has now very largely taken possession of philosophy—thanks to the impact made by Wittgenstein. But this means that today both natural science and philosophy no longer seek truth but only inquire about the correctness of the methods applied and experiment in logic, chiefly in linguistic analysis, quite independently of the question of whether the starting point of this form of thinking corresponds to reality. In any case, reality seems to be inaccessible.

The renunciation of truth itself and a reliance upon what is verifiable and upon the correctness of methods are typical of the modern natural scientific outlook. Man now operates only within his own shell; the intensification of his methods of observation has not led him to become liberated from himself and to press on to the foundation of things; but rather, it has made him instead the prisoner of his own methods, of himself. If literature can be taken as the index of the common mind, we are led to a disquieting diagnosis of man's situation today. The vast literature of absurdity makes very obvious the crisis of our concept of reality. Truth, reality itself, is eluding

man. In the language of the title of the last book
by Günter Grass, man seems to be drugged by
narrow topicality, capable of perceiving only the
tattered rags of reality; he is insecure most of all
at the point where exact science abandons him,
and it is the measure of his abandonment that
first makes him aware of how narrow the slice
of reality is in which science gives him security. It
is true that this feeling has not become universal
by a long way. Even events need time for completion, as Nietzsche observed in his aphorism
about the death of God, when he proclaimed in
moving imagery the absurd man and an absurd reality as consequences of that event, consequences
that he acclaimed with intoxicated passion. Today at the most sensitive points of society, that
is, in literature and its portrayal of man, we are
beginning to find an unexpected verification of
the gruesome visions of Dostoyevsky of a world
without God and of how that world turns into
a madman's dream.[3]

The man who wants to limit himself to what is
knowable in exact terms is caught up in the crisis

---

[3] On Dostoyevsky on this topic, cf. de Lubac, *Drama of Atheist Humanism*, pp. 269–394.

of reality: he beholds the withdrawal of truth. Within himself he hears the cry of faith, which the spirit of the hour has not been able to stifle but has only made all the more dramatic. There is a cry for liberation from the prison of positivism, as there is, too, for liberation from a form of faith that has allowed itself to become a burden instead of the vehicle of freedom. This brings us at last to the point at which the question can be put: How is such a faith to be created? First let us remark: Faith is not a diluted form of natural science, an ancient or medieval preparatory stage that must vanish when the real thing turns up; rather, it is something essentially different. It is not provisional knowledge, although we do use the word in this sense also when we say, for example, "I believe that is so." In such a case "believing" means "being of the opinion". But when we say, "I believe you", the word acquires quite another meaning. It means the same as "I trust you", or even as much as "I rely upon you." The "you" in which I put reliance, provides me with a certainty that is different from but no less than the certainty that comes from calculation and experiment. And it is thus that the word is used in the Christian Credo. The basic form of

Christian faith is not: I believe something, but I believe *you*. Faith is a disclosure of reality that is granted only to him who trusts, loves, and acts as a human being; and as such it is not a derivative of knowledge but is *sui generis*, like knowledge, although it is indeed more basic and more central to our authentically human nature than knowledge is.

This insight has important consequences; and these can be *liberating*, if taken seriously. For this means that faith is not primarily a colossal edifice of numerous supernatural facts, standing like a curious second order of knowledge alongside the realm of science, but an assent to God, who gives us hope and confidence. Obviously this assent to God is not without content: it is confidence in the fact that he has revealed himself in Christ and that we may now live safe in the assurance that God is like Jesus of Nazareth, in the certainty, that is, that God is looking after the world—and me in it. We will have to consider this definition of content more closely in the next chapter. It is already clear, however, that the content is not comparable to a system of knowledge; rather, it represents the form of our trust. For this reason all does not depend, in the last analysis, upon knowing or comprehending every last detail of the separate facets of the faith.[4] Obviously, for the sake of preaching, it is important for the Church to persevere in trying to gain ever fresh understanding even of the details; and there can be no doubt that such a practice will have a progressively enriching effect—as, for example, when it becomes clear that the affirmation that the world proceeded from the Word does not contradict the affirmation that the world formed in an expansion of matter, for each affirmation conveys truth of a totally different kind about the world. And we could follow this principle in respect of all of the problems already mentioned. In all of these efforts, however, one must always bear in mind that every age has its own blind spot, that none can grasp everything, so that in each particular age much has to remain unexplained, because quite simply, the intellectual apparatus is lacking.

This is a situation by no means peculiar to theology. Physics acquires its knowledge, among

---

[4] This is taken for granted again and again in the medieval *summas* also. Cf., for example, Bonaventure, *Sent.* III, d. 25, a. 1, q. 3: "Credere autem omnes articulos explicite et distincte . . . non est de generali fidei necessitate."

other ways, by formulating a hypothesis from many individual observations that explains these phenomena in terms of a whole, sets them in a total context, and permits further advance from the point reached. The more phenomena that are explained, the better the hypothesis. But decisive advance is made only when observations are made that do not fit into any previous hypothesis. It is precisely the errant phenomena that are important. These compel further study, until finally a new context emerges and a new hypothesis is produced that advances beyond the present horizon and gives us a new, more comprehensive view of reality. The same sort of thing happens in thinking about the faith: one is constantly finding oneself in new, unresolved situations, that present trouble but also hope. Our thinking can never completely integrate faith and knowledge, and we must never, from a very understandable impatience, allow ourselves to press on to immature syntheses, which, instead of serving faith well and truly, compromise it. This applies most of all to the particular: the assent of faith as such is concerned with the whole, and only secondarily has it to do with the part, with the separate contents to which faith assents. A man remains a Christian as long as he makes the effort to give the central assent, as long as he tries to utter the fundamental Yes of trust, even if he is unable to fit in or resolve many of the details. There will be moments in life when, in all kinds of gloom and darkness, faith falls back upon the simple, "Yes, I believe you, Jesus of Nazareth; I believe that in you was revealed that divine purpose which allows me to live with confidence, tranquility, patience, and courage." As long as this core remains in place, a man is living by faith, even if for the moment he finds many of the details of faith obscure and impracticable.

Let us repeat: at its core, faith is, not a system of knowledge, but trust. Christian faith is:

the finding of a "you" that upholds me and amid all the unfulfilled—and in the last resort unfulfillable—hope of human encounters gives me the promise of an indestructible love that not only longs for eternity but also guarantees it. Christian faith lives on the discovery that not only is there such a thing as objective meaning but that this meaning knows me and loves me, that I can entrust myself to it like the child who knows that everything he may be wondering about is safe in the "you" of his mother. Thus in the last analysis believing, trusting, and loving are one, and all the theses around which belief revolves are only concrete expressions of the all-embracing about-turn, of the assertion "I believe in you" —of the discovery of God in the countenance of the man Jesus of Nazareth.[5]

---

[5] J. Ratzinger, *Introduction to Christianity*, trans. J. R. Foster (San Francisco: Ignatius Press; Communio Books, 2004), p. 80.

Faith and Existence

In the first chapter we were forced to the conclusion that faith in the Christian sense is not primarily a mysterious system of knowledge, but an existential attitude, a fundamental decision about the direction of life, which we described provisionally by the word "trust". Now we must try to define more clearly this essential core of faith and answer the question: Which direction of existence does a man choose who resolves to tune the instrument of his life to the keynote of faith? This is not an easy question to answer because quite plainly it reaches down into the deeper levels of man's being, into those things that are not always open to the light of day but that permeate and mold the whole of man's being, never themselves amenable to measurement and calculation. All of the big, basic decisions in human life, decisions that go beyond the everyday business of living, can be understood only if one makes an effort to enter to some extent into the movement

from which they emerge—whether this has to
do with a great love or the passion of the inven-
tor or the renunciation of those who dedicate
their lives to a tremendous idea, whether it has
to do with the attitude that is disclosed in the
smile of Buddha or the faith of a Christian.

From what has already been said, another thing
has already become obvious: what faith really
means for a man cannot be represented abstractly;
it can be made visible only by and in men who
have lived out this attitude to its logical conclusion—men like Francis of Assisi, Francis Xavier,
Ignatius of Loyola, Teresa of Avila, Thérèse of
Lisieux, Vincent de Paul, John XXIII—by and
in such men, and basically only thus, can faith
declare clearly what sort of decision it really is.
As such persons show, faith is fundamentally a
particular kind of passion, or, more correctly, a
kind of love that seizes a man and points the
way he must go, even if that way is wearisome.
That way may turn out to be a mountain ascent
that seems folly to the comfortable and narrow-
minded middle-class citizen but, to the one who
has committed himself to the adventure, the one
and only way, which he would not wish to ex-
change for all the comfort in the world. The

Bible, which describes for us the first stage in the history of faith and which is also its enduring measuring rod, points to Abraham as the great exemplary figure, the man who some two thousand years before Christ set out upon the road at the end of which stands the figure of Jesus of Nazareth. This man, whose picture we can but dimly discern from the fragments of tradition preserved for us in the Old Testament, is accredited by the New Testament also as the father of all the faithful, so that Saint Paul can declare categorically that Christians are the children of Abraham. They and they only, in his view, are moving along farther in the same direction as he once took.

Certainly it would have been much easier to form our picture of faith from one of the figures already named, who stand much closer to us in time and in human culture; but perhaps one of the things about biblical faith is precisely this, that it links people not only right across frontiers of language and race, but also across thousands of years. And perhaps it also belongs to faith that it has a history, is a road, the start of which looks so different from the later stages, but which forever remains the one road by which men can travel to God. Perhaps it is important that faith unites us not only with those whom we recognize easily as our intellectual and cultural kinsmen, but also with those who seem at first sight to be quite foreign to us. And the fundamental decision may well become apparent only when we are compelled to see with what a variety of forms and contents it can be allied.

Very different from ours was the way in which Abraham's faith expressed itself. Not only was he necessarily unaware of the person of Jesus Christ, but even monotheism had not become clearly defined in his mind; and Abraham certainly had no belief at all in a life after death. The question about who the God of Abraham really was is disputed today, as it always has been, although extensive discoveries of inscriptions have ruled out excessively revolutionary hypotheses and prove that the biblical tradition is far more reliable than was thought a short time ago. Roughly speaking we can sum up our knowledge as follows. Abraham worshipped the God then well known in the East as El. He was the Creator of all, the highest God in the whole pantheon, and possessed several subsidiary names—the Highest, the Eternal, the Mighty, the All-seeing—and he was worshipped in the most diverse places. Abraham worshipped him as his own family God —and this may have been what distinguished Abraham's piety from that of those around him —as his personal God, who thus became, for his descendants, the God of Abraham and of Israel, until finally, as the God and Father of Jesus Christ, he acquired a new significance. We need not assume that Abraham denied the existence of other gods. The unique element in his belief was the link of which we have spoken. Everyone at that time worshipped El, the Creator, the Highest, and there were family gods everywhere who bore the appropriate family name. But for Abraham, El was his family god, too. He knew that it was he, the Highest, the Lord of All, who had personally called him.[1]

However, this does not comprise the essential content of "the faith of Abraham". What was that faith like? To the modern reader of the Bible, it appears fairly prosaic. Abraham knew that he enjoyed a promise that gave him the prospect of posterity and a country—the two things that

---

[1] Cf. N. Lohfink, *Bibelauslegung im Wandel* (Frankfurt am Main, 1967), pp. 107–28. Further bibliography in H. Haag, *Bibel-Lexikon*, 2nd ed. (Einsiedeln, 1968), p. 14.

were most desirable to men of those times because they assured a future, wealth, and security.
For the sake of this promise, he left the world
of his ancestors and set off into the unknown,
into apparent uncertainty, led on by the certainty
that this was precisely how the future would become his.

It may be that we are disappointed when we
read this very human story. But it will repay us
to take note of what really happened to the man
who was committing himself in this way. He
gave up the present for the sake of what was to
come. He let go of what was safe, comprehensible, calculable, for the sake of what was unknown. And he did this in response to a single
word from God. He had met God and placed all
his future in God's hands; he dared to accept a
new future that began in darkness. The word he
had heard was more real to him than all the calculable things he could hold in his hand. He trusted
in that which he could not yet see and thus became capable of new life, of breaking out of
rigidity. The center of gravity of reality, indeed,
the concept of reality itself, changed. The future
took precedence over the present, the word heard
over comprehensible things. God had become

more important to him than he himself and than the things he could understand. Imprisonment within the calculable and among the goods with which a man surrounds himself was broken, and a new, limitless horizon opened up: a horizon toward the Eternal, toward the Creator. Attachment to the accustomed world around him came to an end, and man's true destination appeared: not his immediate environment, but the whole world, the whole of creation that knows no frontiers but allows itself to be explored until the ultimate foundation of everything has been discovered. This wholeness is represented by the image and the reality of the journey. Abraham is on his way. He no longer belongs to any fixed place and is therefore a stranger and a guest wherever he goes. Scholarship has often interpreted the documents as proving that the ancestors of Israel were nomads and have even made this the explanation of their breakthrough to the God of heaven and a personal God. The nomad—they argue—has no fixed abode on this earth and sees the arch of heaven above as his only constant companion. He can trust himself, not to the gods of any particular country, but only to the God to whom all countries belong; not a local god, but the God who goes with him and knows him personally, is close to him, like a person, from place to place. Many objections are now being made to such an explanation, but what is certain is that Abraham became homeless for the sake of a future, assured him by faith, and that he found a homeland precisely in the certainty of his faith.

What was it, then, that made up the faith of Abraham, which, according to the Bible, is the basic form of all faith, ours included? We are now in a position to say that this faith is essentially related to the future, that it is a promise. It signifies the superordination of the future over the present and the readiness to sacrifice the present for the sake of the future. It signifies life lived in the spirit of trust. It signifies the certainty that it is God who guarantees man his future. Thus it signifies a breaking out of the calculable, everyday world to make contact with what is eternal; it signifies man's interest in eternal things and in the Eternal. It signifies the bold realization that man can have dealings with the Eternal and is not confined within a petty meanness of heart that will not look beyond its immediate surroundings or give itself credit for the greatness that sees that there might be more to human life than bread for tomorrow and money for the day after tomorrow. Finally, we must counter the widely held opinion that such a faith paralyzes us. On the contrary, it sets us moving and introduces responsibility for the future. It teaches us the responsibility of hope, as the New Testament later expresses it in the First Letter of Peter (1 Pet 3:15). Another important feature in the structure of the Christian relationship to God can be learned from the story of Abraham. Abraham heard God's call; he enjoyed some kind of mystical experience, a direct eruption of the divine, which pointed his way for him. This man must have had something of the seer about him, a sensitivity to being, which enlarged his perception beyond the bounds of what is accessible to our normal senses. This extension of the realms of perception, which men in all ages, discontented with their immediate experience, have sought to acquire by artificial means, was obviously enjoyed by him, as by all the great religious geniuses, in a pure, effortless, and original manner. He had a faculty for perceiving the divine.

But this faculty was not reserved to him for the

personal enrichment of his own consciousness; by this experience he became father of his faithful posterity, who from him and through him shared in this broadening of the horizon that was granted to him. Through him they heard and saw what he heard and saw. In this connection, it seems to me, a structural law of biblical faith becomes evident, and this can be formulated thus: God comes to men only through men. The variation that exists in men's capacities for perceiving what lies beyond the bounds of everyday experience is no senseless caprice of nature; rather, it is formative for man's relationship with God and for coexistence among men. In precisely this fashion God makes men interdependent, so that now we may modify and expand our former statement. Just as God comes to men only through men, so men come to one another only through God. A relationship with God is not the private affair of each individual, something into which no one else can or may enter; rather, it is something at once wholly interior and yet wholly public. God has so created man that there are not a plurality of independently coexisting relationships with God, pertaining to the individuals who happen to be there at the time, each one experiencing and grasping God interiorly; it is only in being together that men can come to God, and it is their very search for God that directs them toward one another. The thesis that religion estranges men can be applied only to the corruption of religion, but it is quite untrue as a description of the overall history of religion, especially of that part associated with the name of Abraham.

In all of this we have kept within the confines of the Old Testament. Now we have to ask the question: Is, then, Saint Paul's claim correct, that the faith of Jesus Christ and, above all, faith in Jesus Christ is nothing other than a straight-line continuation of the faith of Abraham? Today, we are very much inclined to say that the faith of Jesus was very like that of Abraham. But faith *in* Jesus seems to form a transition to something totally different and totally new. Saint Paul's assertion that he, too, remained in the line of development from Abraham seems at first to be merely the result of self-justification, designed to prove, by means of the tricks of rabbinic Scripture exegesis, to his Jewish opponents who regarded him as an apostate, that he was no apostate, because in fact faith in Jesus was the only possible and valid

further development in the new situation of the
fundamental spiritual commitment of the Jews.
There can be no doubt that Saint Paul was in-
dulging in a form of self-justification: he wanted
to prove that one could be true to the fathers
only if one now took the step of commitment
to Christ: Judaism would have to turn into Christianity if it wanted to remain true Judaism. And
it is certain that he was subjectively convinced of
the truth of his assertion. But was he correct ob-
jectively? To begin with, it is quite clear that the
Pauline exegesis of the Old Testament follows
a method that is no longer recognized as valid,
so that his interpretation is almost wholly unac-
ceptable to modern philologists and historians.[2]
But does this settle the issue? We must, I think,
go beyond the exegetical details to the basic in-
tuition by which Saint Paul is guided and at least
make an attempt to understand how he and all
whom he convinced were able, nonetheless, to
feel themselves in full continuity with the faith
of Abraham.

---

[2] Cf. R. Bultmann, "Prophecy and Fulfilment", in *Essays* (London:
SCM Press, 1935), pp. 182–208.

To analyze all of this in detail would be a complicated scientific exercise, impossible to fit into the framework of this discussion. We may content ourselves with discovering the basic direction of Saint Paul's thought; and we find that the primary question at issue is that concerning the direction given to existence by the decision of faith, according to the New Testament. The critical passage in which Saint Paul explicitly claims that Christianity is the true continuation of the line descending from Abraham is the fourth chapter of his Letter to the Church in Rome. In this passage Saint Paul asks what was the essence of Abraham's faith and gives the following answer: Against all appearance Abraham believed that God would send him an heir by his wife Sarah, and this heir would make him to be the father of many nations. From the historical point of view, this is undoubtedly to sharpen the facts in a particular direction, but they have been faithfully reproduced in all that is material. For Saint Paul holds to the thesis that the content of Abraham's faith was his hope in posterity (involving hope for a country). To put it more generally, it was hope in a great future; and this motif, concretized in the reference to Sarah and Isaac, is then accentuated in a particular direction by Saint Paul when he says that Abraham believed that he would have an heir from the already dead womb of Sarah—life out of death, as it were. In this way Saint Paul has reached the point where transformation to Christian thought becomes possible. He says in effect that Christian faith trusts in the God who raised Jesus from the dead; it is always a faith that believes in the God who gives life out of death.

For a start, that seems to be an enormous jump. The Christian confession of faith, which in those days was essentially a simple confession of the Resurrection of Jesus from the dead,[3] is identified, in an utterly reckless manner, so it seems to us, with the Credo of Abraham, with his hope for a posterity. In reality it seems that structure and content could not be farther apart. But had Saint Paul not noted that fact also? And can we really impute dishonesty to him, saying that he was

---

[3] Cf. the profession of faith in 1 Corinthians 15:3–8; but in the context the simple christological formula "Jesus is the Christ (or the Lord)" (e.g., 1 Cor 12:3) is an abbreviated profession of faith in the Resurrection, for the fact that Jesus is the Christ is demonstrated by the Resurrection, which was his installation in that office (cf. Rom 1:4).

employing the mere tactics of the apologist, who wanted to justify himself out of Jewish tradition, although he knew full well that he had broken with that tradition? If we accept all this without more ado, we have to continue our investigation farther. I believe, in fact, that, in spite of the undeniably new step that is taken here, there is a certain continuity of direction. How shall we define this? With Abraham it all had essentially to do with his belief that God would give him a future, and this was represented to him under the imagery of a land and posterity.

But is the belief in the God who raised Jesus from the dead anything other than belief in the future that God grants? It seems to me that for Saint Paul, everything depends upon our being able to say that now the promise of a future, of the country of the future, has acquired a full and clearly defined form. Faith in the risen Christ is nothing other than the faith of Abraham—the promise of a future and of a country. That is how we take our bearings. But this future is understood in a radically different way. It strides across the frontier of death, which is the real antithesis to man's attachment to the future. Man has been made so that he cannot live without a future.

Between the two world wars a radio play about the end of the world was broadcast in America. It was so realistic that many people thought the end really was imminent, and a great number of suicides occurred. People took their lives so as not to have to die, as Emmanuel Mounier so aptly said—a piece of absurdity that nonetheless clearly expressed the real makeup of man. Without a future, even the present becomes unbearable, and for this reason we do not dare, as a rule, to tell the incurably sick of their condition. Nothing is so unbearable for man as to have no future.

Suicide as a flight from death, however, is but the lurid illumination of the paradox of human existence in general. It is oriented wholly toward the future, and yet all future is in the end snatched away from it, for its end is death. In this contradiction between being oriented toward the future and having the future snatched away from it lies the real melancholy of human existence; and this is all the more palpable the more alertly a man lives his life and the more radically he perceives death truly as death and as his ultimate end. In this respect, the memoirs of Simone de Beauvoir are a shattering witness to the situation of the man who has become aware of himself in all his contradiction.

> If of an evening I happened to have drunk a glass too many, it could easily happen that I wept buckets. My old longing for the absolute awoke; I discovered afresh the vanity of human striving and the menacing nearness of death. . . . Sartre denies that truth is to be found in wine and in tears. In his opinion, alcohol made me melancholy, and I was disguising my condition with metaphysical reasons. I held, on the contrary, that alcohol removes the defenses and controls that normally protect us from unbearable certainties and, so, compels me to face up to them. Today, I believe that in a privileged case like mine life embraces two truths, between which there is no choice, and one has to face both of them: the zest for life and dread of the end.[4]

Anyone who has bravely faced up to the knowledge of himself knows, too, that for men posterity alone cannot provide the land of the future. Conversely, it would be interesting to allude to what Simone de Beauvoir tells about

---

[4] This quotation is translated from the German edition of the memoirs of Simone de Beauvoir published by Rowohlt. Cf. the article by H. J. Lauter, "Der ungläubige Mensch im Angesicht des Todes", *Sein und Sendung* 1 (1969): 255–60.

her acquaintance, the communist Nizan, who officially preached the doctrine that the future is something men find in their work for a coming classless society but in private was utterly filled with dissatisfaction with this solution and felt shattered by the eeriness of the absence of a real future for man behind the deceitful façade of the promise of a collective future.[5] The cry that rises up from mankind for a future is not answered by an anonymous collectivity. Man longs for a future in which he himself will be included.

Abraham's hope had to be superseded or, rather, filled out in content to the extent that man discovered himself. Faith in the God of Jesus Christ means faith in the God who still opens up, really and truly, a future behind the wall of death. Only if that happens is the future truly promised. Thus, structurally, faith in the God who raised Jesus from the dead is the exact continuation of the faith of Abraham, which in a new phase of human history for the first time gave to this faith its full weight, its full meaning and true significance. All the basic elements of this faith, which

---

[5] Simone de Beauvoir, *The Force of Circumstance*, trans. Richard Howard (London: Andre Deutsch; Weidenfeld & Nicolson, 1965).

we have already tried to trace, remain intact and acquire a new aspect from this new concept of the future. Today, too, faith signifies a breaking out of the visible and calculable into a wider sphere. Today, it still means breaking open the horizon and reaching out across all frontiers. And even today it signifies setting out upon a journey and going beyond that false sense of being settled which holds a man to what is "small but my own", thus depriving him of true greatness. In our day, too, faith signifies an inversion of values, a resetting of the weights and measures of existence in terms of the standard of the future. Not what is useful for the moment, but what is conformed to eternity is appropriate to man. What is conformed to eternity: that is what is worthy of lasting. That is a man who has become such that one need no longer wish to get rid of him soon. That is therefore also precisely a man who has become human and humane. A man who is able to give something; a man who does not stand in the way of others, but means something to them, a man whom one can love.

By putting this standard of "what is conformed to eternity", of what is worthy of eternity, under the microscope, as it were, and analyzing its

details, we have in the process provided the answer to an objection that we have already en-
countered in our inquiry into the faith of Abraham and that appears more sharply when directed
at the Christian faith. Does this kind of orientation toward a future that transcends death not
imply an escape into the hereafter and a devalu-
ation of earthly life? Does it not tempt us to in-
activity and a false belief in consolation through
compensations to come, encouraging us to leave
everything to a future judge, when we ought
to be fighting passionately for justice here and
now? There can be no doubt that such a flight
and such a passivity have resulted and do result from biblical faith; Saint Paul himself had
to take issue with this misinterpretation.[6] From
the very beginning he saw that it was a misinterpretation. It is precisely when a man possesses
an eternal future, which determines his present,
that this present acquires an un-heard-of, almost
unbearable, significance. Once again, Simone de
Beauvoir saw these facts with astonishing clear-
sightedness, precisely in terms of her conviction
of death as an irrevocable end. She writes:

---

[6] Cf. 1 Thess 4:11; 2 Thess 3:10ff.; Eph 4:28.

Yet I loathe the thought of annihilating myself quite as much now as I ever did. I think with sadness of all the books I've read, all the places I've seen, all the knowledge I've amassed and that will be no more. All the music, all the paintings, all the culture, so many places: and suddenly nothing. . . . Nothing will have taken place, I can still see the hedge of hazel trees flurried by the wind and the promises with which I fed my beating heart while I stood gazing at the gold mine at my feet: a whole life to live. The promises have all been kept. And yet, turning an incredulous gaze toward that young and credulous girl, I realize with stupor how much I was gypped.[7]

These are the final words of her memoirs. They express the abysmal melancholy of a present without a future, the most beautiful elements in which appear in the end as deception. Faith in the risen Christ, in the God who gives life beyond death, creates responsibility, gives substance to the present, because it then falls under the measure of the eternal.

We could continue reflecting upon the basic elements of the faith of Abraham and upon the modification and the development it under-

---

[7] Beauvoir, *Force of Circumstance*, from the last two pages.

goes in the Christian faith. Take, for example, the notion of pilgrimage, of being always on a journey, now interiorized as the readiness to allow oneself to be changed, to move forward,[8] to remain open, as the readiness, also, to accept the alien status of the wanderer, who appears to those entrenched in this world and its affairs as a contemptible stranger—today more than ever. Christians, who have suffered trial and torture under totalitarian powers, tell how they were constantly being reproached with not being fully in this world: they always have a Lord, a task, a standard, that transcends the party and its norms. The destiny of the pilgrim, who never quite settles down but belongs to a wider sphere, becomes supremely obvious in such a context. And how much could we not infer from this! The necessity of resisting all totalitarianism—a logical consequence of faith; the universality of mankind that makes the striving for peace among men an inescapable task for Christians; and many other things as well.

But let us turn instead to one last question that arises from the Pauline text we have taken

---

[8] Cf. the fine expositions by D. von Hildebrand in *Transformation in Christ: On the Christian Attitude* (San Francisco, 2001), pp. 3–29.

as our starting point, for an objection of some weight can be raised against what has already been argued. One might say: Very well, then, the archetypal form of faith as faith in ultimate life, presented to us in the risen Christ, who fulfills all God's promises to us, does remain in line with Abraham's faith: trust in the future that teaches us to endure the present. But what has been made out of this? What has Saint Paul made out of it? With him has this simple Credo not already been remolded into the complicated doctrine of justification, which then embraced the whole of Christology and, since the Reformation, has split Western Christendom? Obviously this question concerning Saint Paul must be extended to cover the whole history of dogma. In the first chapter we made a few comments on this topic; we may now be allowed to confine ourselves, therefore, to the remolding of faith in the Resurrection into the doctrine of redemption or of justification. I must confess that I have never found the connection between the doctrine of justification and the promise of the future so clearly expressed as in a passage from Albert Camus' novel *The Fall*, wherein a fictional hero makes a moving self-confession that reflects the whole problem of man today. For him, God has long since become obsolete, and so he wastes few words on him, but one of the passages where he is mentioned seems to me of the utmost importance for the thoughtful Christian.

> Believe me, religions are on the wrong track the moment they start to moralize and fulminate commandments. God is not needed to create guilt or to punish. Our fellow-men suffice, aided by ourselves. You were speaking of the Last Judgement. Allow me to laugh respectfully. I shall wait for it resolutely, for I have known what is worse, the judgment of men. . . .
>
> So what? Well, God's sole usefulness would be to guarantee innocence, and I am inclined to see religion rather as a huge laundering venture —as it was once but briefly, for exactly three years, and it wasn't called religion.[9]

A God who really was God (so the speaker is saying) should not have to give a single command or make a single prohibition, should not threaten and watch over men, but should defend and forgive them.

In reality, the promise of an eternal future, of which we spoke earlier, can be not only redemp-

---

[9] Albert Camus, *The Fall*, in *The Collected Fiction of Albert Camus* (London: Hamish Hamilton, 1960), p. 292.

tive for men, but annihilating and menacing also. For the thought that all his doings will be measured according to the measure of eternity determines more than the passing moment; rather, it passes across the frontier of death. For the man who takes it seriously, this thought is bound to appear frightening, and he may well flee from the prospect of this future and prefer to accept the absence of any future rather than submit to the demands that the future would make upon him. Thus we find ourselves facing a unique contradiction. On the one hand, man needs to have a future beyond death, while, on the other hand, he cannot bear the thought. If the promise of a future is to be truly hope or "redemption" for men, the measure of eternity must be forgiveness as well. Faith in the future, by which we mean Abraham's faith as fulfilled in Christ, is promise and hope and the true offer of a future only because it promises also a land of forgiveness. To this extent, the doctrine of redemption or justification is only an aspect of the faith of Abraham, of confidence in the land of the future that God opens up to us beyond the frontier of death.

In conclusion, let us ask once again: What, in the light of the Bible, is "faith"? And let us again affirm clearly: It is not a system of semi-knowledge, but an existential decision—it is life in terms of the future that God grants us, even beyond the frontier of death. This is the attitude and orientation that gives life its weights and measures, its ordinances, and its very freedom. Certainly a life lived by faith resembles more an expedition up a mountain than a quiet evening spent reading in front of the fire; but anyone who embarks upon this expedition knows and experiences more and more that the adventure to which it invites us is worthwhile.

Faith and Philosophy

There are various reasons for the dilemma in which the Christian faith finds itself today. One of the most important, however, is that faith has been left in the lurch by philosophy and suddenly finds itself, so to speak, in a vacuum. In ancient times and in the Middle Ages, one of the things that helped men to find faith was that philosophy provided them with a picture of the world in which faith could find a meaningful place. Even at the beginning of modern times, philosophy created a kind of transitional field between the exact sciences, the method of which necessarily excluded God from study, and the authentic realm of faith. Despite many differences, there still remained a common root of more or less generally accepted metaphysics that spoke of God as the Creator of all things, as the spiritual and intelligent foundation of the universe, thus providing a conceptual basis for the notion of a God who reveals himself.

Since Immanuel Kant the unity of philosophical thought has more and more become disrupted. The thing to suffer most has been the reliable certainty that man can feel his way, by solid intellectual argument, behind the realm of physics to the being of things and to their ultimate cause. This certainty has almost wholly vanished. Obviously there were and are philosophers who still consider such a metaphysic to be possible and who, in sharp antithesis to Kant and his followers, wish to assure it a place in human thought. But even such philosophers cannot put the clock back. Their philosophy can no longer be presented as *the* philosophy that everyone accepts without demur and that can therefore be made the presupposition of all else. Their thought represents, in fact, *one* philosophy among others, and this greatly reduces the value of anything that tries to build upon it. Even where metaphysics is still practiced, the former situation cannot be reinstated. Philosophy no longer exists—only philosophies. Thus, acceptance of a philosophy signifies, no longer assent to the common heritage of the human spirit, but merely the taking up of a position that may be reasonable but that aligns one against other equally reasonable positions. There is thus no point at which faith can any longer link up securely with human thought. If it tries to do so, it is clutching at empty air.

The first to seek a way out of this situation was the Evangelical theologian Schleiermacher, a contemporary of Kant. For more than a century his solution molded the course of Evangelical theology in Germany and exerted an influence in Catholic circles also. Schleiermacher maintained that there are in man various, noninterchangeable forms of contact with the world and of grasping reality, each with its own weight and importance. Understanding, will, and emotion are the three provinces of the human mind, and none is derived from any other, and none can be transmuted into any other. The understanding is correlated to science, the will to ethics, emotion to religion, which he defined as beholding and sensing the universe or as sensitivity to and appreciation of the infinite. Later he was to define it as the feeling of utter dependence. The rationalism of the Enlightenment had tried to reduce religion to one or two universally self-evident propositions. Behind the positive religions it wanted to reconstruct a religion of pure reason, which would

unite all men. This artificial edifice, a religion
synthetically manufactured in the retort of reflection, had vanished like a soap bubble at the impact of Kant's critique. By his notion, Schleiermacher arrived at the independence of religion
from the efforts of metaphysics, from the operation of pure reason in general: religion was experience, the experience of the infinite and of the
dependence of men upon it. Thus it was something *sui generis*, completely independent of meta-
physical reflection, and an autonomous sphere of
the human spirit. In this way a feeling for the
historically developed religions was re-aroused.
Our aim cannot be an artificially constructed religion. For Schleiermacher the truth was, rather,
that religion is to be found only in the religions
that, from time to time, have emerged as living
structures, the meaning and teachings of which
can be understood only through an attitude of
reverence and of commitment.[1]

---

[1] Cf. K. E. Welker, *Die grundsätzliche Beurteilung der Religionsgeschichte
bei Schleiermacher* (Leiden and Cologne, 1965), which gives a bibliography. On this question, I am indebted to valuable suggestions made
by G. Söhngen in his lecture series on the philosophy of religion,
during the session 1949–1950.

The advance represented by this thesis is impossible to overlook, but it produced serious and problematic consequences for the Christian faith. If what Schleiermacher said is true, the characteristic quality of religion is the inexpressibility of a feeling by which the infinite is perceived. The contents in which religion expresses itself become no more than forms of piety that in the end are purely secondary—stammering attempts to present in words something that remains forever inexpressible. The important thing in the language of religion would not, then, be the "what" but only the "that", for which reason Schleiermacher was also able to say that the truly pious need not know Holy Scripture—indeed, he would be better to write his own. That is to say, the place of faith is taken over by piety, or, in other words, in place of an objective partner who comes to meet me, who binds and yet frees me, we find the identity of the subject who senses the eternal. This all becomes particularly clear in Schleiermacher's verdict on Jesus Christ, whom he portrays as the man with the highest and purest sensitivity to God. Jesus *is* not God, but *possesses* the highest awareness of God.

Consciousness never spills over in the direction of being, or vice versa; consciousness takes the place of being. The frontier of subjectivity never opens up, and thus Schleiermacher remains a prisoner of the Kantian diversion into the subject.

If we look more closely, we can see that in this way religion would indeed find justification, but not faith. Above all, what is specifically Christian would disappear, even if Schleiermacher tries to make room for it by portraying Christianity as the highest and most mature form of religious consciousness. One could accept the fact that once the modern age had really emerged, Christianity would have to accept this retreat, that it would have to fit into this relativist system; one could be of the opinion that this is the only form in which, in modern times, Christianity could make sense even to itself. Many, indeed, were of this opinion—an opinion that is taking on a new lease of life today, even in Catholic circles. But one could also be of the opinion that this would be to lose something specifically Christian, that thus the very thing that Christianity wants to carry on into history as its very own would vanish. In that case, with due respect, criticism of Schleiermacher's achievement would be in order. The Berlin theologian had always had opponents, but the world had to wait for quite some time for a large-scale, historically effective protest. This came, for the first time really, from Karl Barth, who at the beginning of the twenties of this century first sounded the trumpet against Schleiermacher, thus ushering in the end of the theology of the nineteenth century, the end of the period dominated by Schleiermacher. Barth's point of departure is, among other things, the affirmation already described, that today faith can no longer find a point of contact with philosophy but seems to stand over against it, in a vacuum. By his reference to feeling, Schleiermacher had tried to remove the awkwardness of this situation and had made an effort to find a human anchorage for religion among the ruins of reason. But he had done this at the expense of emptying faith of all content, as we have seen. In his early period, Barth reacted against all this with passionate emphasis. Faith requires no point of contact at all with reason; it cannot have any; it dare not have any. According to Barth, the error of Schleiermacher, as of a large part of Catholic tradition, consists in their seeking a point of contact, doing violence in the process to both faith and reason.

With Barth, therefore, emerged a vision of great boldness, which excited and inspired the men of those days: faith is not something explicable, grasped by the reason at the end of a long and wearisome chain of argument, but the lightning of divine action, which falls upon us and subdues us by its might, without our assistance and against our calculations. Whoever wants to prove it has already betrayed it. Faith, in reality, is sheer contradiction, that which we cannot explain, because it explains us and precedes us; it is the antecedent of all our intellection. It is the act of God upon us and has no point of contact. This idea made it possible for Barth to be at once radically modern and radically believing. Now he was able to say goodbye to all the attempts to explain God, the miracles of Jesus and his divinity, all the labors of apologetics, and say: "The cry of the rebel against this God is closer to the truth than all the arts of those who want to justify him."[2] If faith is the paradoxical dealing

---

[2] Karl Barth, *The Epistle to the Romans* (London: Oxford Univ. Press, 1933).

of God with us, it is clear that man can never at any point prove it in human terms. Proofs, from the start, are a flight from faith. It follows, therefore, that man on his own can only be, and must be, an atheist, having no organ correlated to the divine. His religion is but a form of self-interest, not a preparation for faith. One can calmly accede to the most radical of the moderns and need no longer bother with all the subtleties of apologetic. Once again the Christian enjoys solidarity with his fellowmen who cannot see God and do not hold with the proofs of the theologians. But this resolute affirmation of the godless situation of the modern mind is conjoined with a complete faith. Once again the word of God declares itself as that which confronts the human spirit; it is no longer a form of our consciousness, but that very thing which approaches us from outside and seizes us. In contrast to Schleiermacher's retreat into subjective piety, faith again emerges in its objectivity and its freedom from human control.

With this strident roll of drums, modern theology was inaugurated. The most wide-awake and critical minds (among them Rudolf Bultmann) forsook the liberal camp and attached themselves to Barth, because this allowed them to be both radically critical and radically Christian.[3] If we survey the theological situation today, nothing of that promising beginning seems to remain. In reality, the early writings of Barth held the key to the present theological situation, which cannot be understood apart from him. If we examine things closely, we can see that from Barth's starting point two completely different roads can be followed. For the starting point itself faces in two directions: on the one hand, it embraces the man who is totally abandoned to his profanity, who is able to know nothing of God, and who is true to himself only if he becomes an atheist; on the other hand, it embraces the self-sufficient word of God set against this profanity, a word that recreates faith but abrogates religion. First of all, the possibility arises of elaborating along the second direction, of unfolding afresh the whole content of faith, under the shelter of this paradox, so to speak. This was the road Barth himself took in writing his *Church Dogmatics*. A kind of neo-orthodoxy emerged— impressive, but, precisely by reason of its lack of

---

[3] Cf. J. M. Robinson, *A New Quest of the Historical Jesus* (London: SCM Press, 1959). (In German translation: *Kerygma und historischer Jesus* [Zurich, 1960], pp. 59f.)

rational foundation, questionable. Alongside this ran another road, that pioneered by Bultmann, to be followed by Bonhoeffer, then Dorothee Solle and the theologians of the death of God. Today one might argue in the following manner: Intrinsically man is an atheist. He knows absolutely nothing about God. Anything he does affirm of God originates in evil. Religion—even the Christian "religion"—is superstition and idolatry. Within Christianity, Barth had made a distinction between faith and religion, damning the latter as the work of man, extolling the former as the act of God. The question remains: What is it in Christianity that truly is not religion? If faith is detached from religion, must it not become reduced in the end to an intangible formality, to the pinpoint of paradox? In the end, must not all the content of the paradox be swallowed up in the condemnation of religion? Or is it not ultimately quite impossible to maintain the paradox? Is it not the final religious illusion, through the back door of which the whole apparatus of religion sneaks back in? And in the end, does not logic leave none but the atheist standing?

In this connection, it is interesting to observe how at an early date missionaries complained about the effects of the theology of Karl Barth. They said that, in the end, all that was left was a critique of religion that played into the hands of the Marxist critics of religion, while the sledge-hammer of paradox then became utterly useless. In the field of theology, development followed a slower course but ran, nonetheless, in the same direction, so that today the mighty *Dogmatics* of Barth is very largely a dead letter, whereas the other side to his starting point has become increasingly autonomous. The paradox of the word of God that finds no human point of contact vanishes; all that is left is a man without religion, a man who cannot and may not inquire about God. Hence there is inaugurated "theology after the death of God", which vainly tries to give the impression that it still has a job to do. The Jesus of history, whom it tries to see as God's representative and in whom it seeks for a justification of its own efforts, is an invention all too easily disposed of: a man retrospectively exalted as a human hero or made the patron of all revolutionaries, while one forgets that this man himself summed up the whole direction of his life in the word "Father", which he applied to the God whom his later disciples have meantime declared to be dead.

Thus the net effect of the fresh theological start of the twenties turns out to be appallingly negative, in spite of all the treasures that have been heaped up during the past fifty years and that are open to later interpretation. The starting point itself, the attempt to master the tricky situation by means of paradox and to declare the vacuum to be the only proper place for faith to inhabit, has been discredited. In spite of all that has been said, theology requires its point of contact in the searching and the questioning of the human spirit. It cannot be erected upon an intellectual void. Admittedly, this lands us once again in all the distress indicated in our first reflections on the subject. There is no longer a common philosophical certainty, unless it be the certainty, shared by all modern philosophies, that there is no certainty beyond the sphere of the exact sciences. Does this mean that we have come to the end of the road as far as a philosophical answer to the question about God is concerned? What *are* we to do now?

I do not presume to possess a recipe that will

clarify the whole problem. Were there such a recipe, it would have been discovered long ago by someone else. It is clear that we cannot avoid careful analysis of every single component in the modern mind if we are to discover whether there is in that mind a place for faith and what that faith looks like. In addition, it is clear also that the modern mind places us before a new situation in which man has to reassess his position within the whole of reality and has to ask anew what attitude he must adopt toward himself and the whole of reality. Finally, it seems clear to me that we cannot avoid asking whether, in this fundamentally altered situation of man, faith still has any function at all or whether it is to be reckoned among those phenomena for which there is no room in life today. Thus we cannot simply proceed on the assumption that Christianity, too, must by all means still be accommodated somewhere, rather, we have seriously to ask whether our efforts may not have meanwhile become superfluous and whether our dilemma has reached the enormous proportions it has because we are trying to save something that evolution has already bypassed. In this respect, the so-called "God is dead theology" seems to me to be not nearly radical enough. It does not contemplate giving up the site for which, on its own diagnosis, the lease has long since expired.

What is the true state of affairs? For a start, we must concede unequivocally that one cannot prove the necessity of God for man in the same manner as one would verify experimentally, say, the quantum theory of Max Planck. Saying this, however, we touch the real root of the philosophical movement of the whole modern period and the foundation of its present dilemma, which has led in practice to a widespread destruction of philosophy in general. For all the contradictions by which it seems to have been hopelessly fragmented, philosophical thought today is guided by a common basic tendency: by the attempt to turn philosophy into an exact science, to practice it *more geometrico*, as Spinoza put it. This endeavor becomes all the more fateful for philosophy, the more the exact natural sciences develop and express themselves in a method, for in the same measure does the distance between the scientific quality of philosophy and that of the natural sciences increase. The universality, the generality, the communicability and demonstrability of the constantly advancing natural sciences, which never cease to increase their common treasure of assured knowledge, confront philosophy, which, despite all efforts, has been utterly torn in shreds and whose practitioners understand one another less and less, with scarcely two heads to be found among them who agree. This damages the prestige of philosophy, and it is always making fresh starts, but these now seek, by rigorous limitation of scope and clear definition of method, to make philosophy "positive" in the sense of natural science, which is limited to what is given and amenable to verification. The history of philosophy since Kant tells of a continuous succession of such attempts. Kant himself tried to take a decisive step in this direction by debunking metaphysics as "precritical" philosophy, by pushing the "thing in itself", that is, the essential depth of the real, out onto the edge of philosophy, to become that which is unknowable by man. To put it very roughly, he reduced philosophy to the analysis of the conditions of the possibility of human knowledge, to the elucidation of the laws of human consciousness.

Ever since then, this verdict has determined the fate of philosophy, the scope of which has progressively diminished, even though men like Fichte, Hegel, and Schelling did try once again to break through into the realm of total reality, more boldly and pretentiously than ever before, taking their stand upon absolute reason and seeking to comprehend the reason of being as a whole. But it was this very attempt to grasp being as reason that led in Feuerbach and Marx to its transformation into the opposite: to the denial of a reason permeating all things, to the absolutization of matter, allied in Marx to the affirmation that there is no such thing as enduring truth, which would depend upon the former spiritual definition of things. Reality, then, is change, and man's task is to intervene in this process of change and himself create truth. From being the measure of man, truth now became his creature. To prevent sheer caprice and a war of all against all from ensuing, the controlling power of the party was required. Philosophy then became a function of the party—party philosophy. Anyone who could not go along with this new realism turned back all the more resolutely to Kant and found the walls of his own consciousness more and more impenetrable. There was no longer any way out to the reality that lay beyond consciousness.

It is not necessary for us here to follow the devious paths of philosophical thought, which remained a prisoner within its own starting point and yet was never able to give up its claim to inquire into the whole of reality. The sobering result of all of these attempts was simply that, a century and a half after Kant's *Critique of Pure Reason*, philosophy still had not become an exact science but, rather, found itself more fragmented and more helpless than ever. The road into the party is not a philosophical route, but what else is there? In this situation, Heidegger resolutely called for a retreat behind Socrates. Being was to be perceived, he asserted, only in the voice of the poets. Sartre, in his own fashion, did the same thing: he put his philosophy on the stage. Today the voices of the existentialists are becoming softer and softer, and the stage is being taken over by the followers of Wittgenstein and the structuralists, insofar as the latter are not being shouted down by the Maoist party-men. The name of Wittgenstein stands for the program whose aim is to turn philosophy once and for all into an exact science by causing it to renounce completely all attempts to solve unanswerable questions about reality and to confine itself to the analysis of human language. Even the attempt to elucidate consciousness seems, according to this program, to be too ambitious;

that which is immediately accessible is merely the expression of consciousness in language, and it is the structures of language that are elucidated. This is a feasible task and one that yields much valuable knowledge. But it does not fulfill the function of philosophy, for man has to go on living and fill his life with a meaning that extends beyond the bounds of arbitrary theorizing and is to be found in responsibility toward reality. If today the youth of the West are protesting against science that is philosophically neutral, and, conversely, the youth of the East, insofar as they are allowed scope to do so, are opposing party science, this represents a convergence of movements, which shows how the opposed ways of East and West are astonishingly one in their ultimate human failure.

Something of very great import is revealed by all of this: the moment that philosophy finally submits to the canon of the exact sciences and tries to fit into the last available space in the system of modern thought, this completion of the system leads to absurdity. Where exact thinking is the rule, we are left with the *homme absurde*, who protests (as has happened): "A life that does not know that it has no meaning makes little

sense."⁴ A man who can no longer transcend the
limits either of his consciousness or of his speech
fundamentally can no longer speak of anything
at all. The language of formulae, of the technical calculus is the only thing that is left for
him. Much as that might be, if man possesses
some reason for these formulae, how appallingly
little it is if there is nothing more besides. To
make positivity an absolute, as Comte prophe-
sied would happen, makes not only inquiry about
God, but inquiry about man and reality in general quite impossible. In the process, this turns
existence itself into a luxury positivism cannot
afford. What does become evident, however, is
that today we are not standing before an isolated
crisis of theology, which alone can no longer find
a place for itself in a sufficiently well-filled universe. We are facing, rather, a fundamental crisis in reality in general, and the displacement of
theology is but the most concrete expression of
the fundamental dilemma of existence into which
we have been precipitated by the triumphant
advance of positivist thought. Positivism, exact

---

⁴ Quoted by P. H. Simon, *Ce que je crois* (Paris: Grasset, 1966), esp.
chap. 4, where we find a masterly analysis entitled "Literature".

scientific method, is unbelievably useful and absolutely necessary for the mastery of the problems of ever-developing humanity. But positivism as a philosophy of life is intolerable and the
end of humanity.

Seen in this light, inquiry about God is not
the forlorn effort of the obsolete world that is
trying to keep itself alive after its time has run
out, but the most necessary thorn in the flesh
of our minds, forcing us constantly to search
for ourselves and to expose ourselves to the
full responsibility of being human—a responsibility that cannot be reduced to the language of
calculus. The triumphantly sober sentence with
which Wittgenstein concludes his *Tractatus logico-
philosophicus*: "What we cannot speak about we
must consign to silence" is only apparently logical. The *logos*, the intellect of man reaches farther than formal logic. Man simply has to speak
about the inexpressible if he would speak about
himself. He must reflect precisely on the incalculable if his thinking is to touch the sphere of the
truly human. Ludwig von Ficker, indeed, showed
good taste by declining to print the *Tractatus* in
the *Brenner*, the newspaper of which he was edi-
tor and which purported to be an organ serving

the cause of progressive thinking that was concerned about the humanity of man.[5]

Let us draw a final conclusion. If empirical
thinking alone is unable to disclose the whole of
reality to man, if restriction to its method leads
to closing the door on reality and to the absurd
man, for good or ill we will have to accept the
fact that human thought runs in several channels.
Then philosophy will have to surrender its am-
bition to be exact in the same way as physics and
chemistry are exact. Philosophy will have to seek
its continuity and its universality in something
other than an ever-growing heap of commonly
accepted formulae. And it does possess a continuity and universality of its own that is in many
respects greater than that of the natural sciences.
The works of Plato, of Augustine, of Thomas
Aquinas, of Pascal, and of Hegel are as topical
today as when they were written. The works of

---

[5] Cf. the informative exposition that Ficker himself gives of his
relationship to Wittgenstein and that also provides one of the best
comprehensive appraisals there is of Wittgenstein's aims and work: L.
von Ficker, *Denkzettel und Danksagungen*, ed. F. Seyr (Munich, 1967),
pp. 199–221, esp. from p. 208. Cf. also the review of the state of the
discussion about Wittgenstein provided by U. Steinvorth in *Hochland*
61 (1969): 569–72. On the questions raised by this, see especially
J. Möller, *Glauben und Denken im Widerspruch? Philosophische Fragen an
die Theologie der Gegenwart* (Munich, 1969).

the pioneers of the natural sciences are but the prehistory, now swallowed up in the whole story of which they were the beginning. The works of Plato and of Pascal are not prehistory but as contemporary now as on the day they were written. What does this signify? That philosophical thought must first rediscover itself in a changed situation; that in a certain respect it will always have something to do with "faith", that is, with the attempt to reflect, to purify, and to universalize spiritual fundamental judgments in responsible thought.

With that we have reached the point at which the problem of faith and philosophy can be taken up afresh and developed farther. Here we must come to a halt. All we can do is point the direction. The philosophical homelessness of faith indicates, not its obsolescence, but the general crisis in thought in which we live. Faith will have to come through this trial in frank communication with every other serious effort that is being made to find a new philosophy of the world and of man. It could make no worse mistake than to add its own voice to the positivist choir, for then it would betray the specific function it is supposed to fulfill on behalf of mankind instead of helping man to find himself. Faith must persevere in reaching out for the whole of reality and, in so doing, maintain the fundamentality of the problem of truth, which will not allow itself to be cast adrift by positivism. It will have to recognize its own philosophical responsibility and inquire ever afresh about its own intelligibility. As things are, faith cannot count on a bundle of philosophical certainties that lead up to faith and support it. It will be compelled, rather, to prove its own legitimacy in advance by reflecting on its own inner reasonableness and by presenting itself as a reasonable whole, which can be offered to men as a possible and responsible choice. To say this is to imply that faith must clearly adjust itself to an intellectual pluralism that cannot ever be reversed and, within this intellectual climate, must present itself as a comprehensible offer of meaning, even if it can find no prolegomena in a commonly accepted philosophical system. That means, in the end, that the meaning which man needs becomes accessible in any case only through a decision for a meaningful structure. It may not be proved, but it can be seen as meaningful. The situation of faith and of those who believe thus becomes more arduous than it used to be. But let us not deceive ourselves. Anyone who inherited more than a set of customs must always have known that effort would always be demanded of him. In no other way is the adventure of human life to be mastered. It is the very severity of this adventure that makes it beautiful.

The Future of the World
Through the Hope of Men

In his *Confessions*,[1] Saint Augustine examines the remarkable phenomenon of time and tries to fathom its essence. In the course of the penetrating analysis he makes, he stumbles upon an astonishing fact: that there is no such thing as the present as a delimitable entity. For, the moment I set about calling something the present, that present is already past and has given way to a new moment. To be precise, the present is merely the extensionless point of division between the past and the future. The notion of the present arises entirely from our consciousness comprehending a piece of time as a unity and thinking of this as its

---

This manuscript was prepared as one of a series of lectures designed to help expound the Pastoral Constitution on the Church in the Modern World, produced by Vatican II. The essay attempts to clarify the speculative background to chapter 3 of the first part of the constitution.

[1] *Confessions* XI, 13 and 17–end. Cf. the analysis of the text by Hans Urs von Balthasar, *Das Ganze im Fragment: Aspekte der Geschichtstheologie* (Einsiedeln, 1963), pp. 21–25.

present moment. Thus the present is a psychic, an intellectual phenomenon. Hence, the present is different from individual to individual, because the segment that each comprehends as his "now" is quite different from that of others. Augustine searches deeper at this point and asks: If this is how things are, what is truly real? The past is no more, the future not yet, and the present is something we create ourselves by uniting past and future in a whole. What, then, is reality? We do not wish to follow up these considerations any further here, although it is useful now and again to call them to mind in order to impress upon our minds the problems inherent in our approach to what is real and that we imagine to be so solid and sure.

Let us confine ourselves to the first observation: the present is a creation of human consciousness, comprehending past and future in one "now". As we have said, this means that the present can have very different accents. There are times when the present is replete with the past, as in the late phases of a culture that looks no longer forward but backward. Thus, most likely, was the present conceived in the Church before the Second Vatican Council. Theology seemed to have thought its way through everything, piety to have practiced and crystalized everything that could possibly be done and formulated; every space had been filled up with the data of tradition, just like a church building that is packed with altars, pictures, and testimonies to the piety of former generations. When such a state of affairs has been reached, either the present, which in any case is now indistinguishable from the past, becomes engulfed in the past, or there takes place a kind of explosion, which is designed to make more space—although in the process, it must be admitted, precious and sound things are thrown out along with much that really is soiled and tattered.[2] Again, there are other periods so preoccupied with the pressures of the present moment that they find it impossible to look either forward or backward. And, finally, there are periods in which the whole weight of interest lies in the future and in which the present is completely filled up by expectation of the morrow.

---

[2] Cf. the instructive exposition by A. Grillmeier, "Die Reformidee des II. Vatikanischen Konzils und ihre Forderung an uns", in *Wahrheit und Verkündigung*, ed. L. Scheffczyk, W. Dettloff, and R. Heinzmann, pp. 1467–88, esp. 1469ff. (Paderborn, 1967), an essay for M. Schmaus on his seventieth birthday.

This was the kind of present enjoyed by early Christianity, which saw the whole of an over-loaded past history as fundamentally ended and which lived wholly by expectation of what was to come—the new world to be established when Christ came again. Of the same sort, but in a to-tally different mode, is our own time, for it sees all the past very largely as but the prologue to a completely new age to which mankind is ad-vancing with ever-quickening steps.

Today, we most certainly have the impression that we are living at a tremendous turning point in the evolution of mankind, at a turning point compared with which the transition from Mid-dle Ages to modern times seems as nothing; and even the revolution inaugurated by the move-ment of the peoples, which divided antiquity from the Middle Ages, seems to have scarcely any significance compared to the revolution we are experiencing today, for it is comparable in its effects only to the really catastrophic revolutions in the evolution of mankind. Perhaps never be-fore has the element of *time* or *development* struck men in so spectacular a way as it does today. Any-one who has been awake to the events of the past thirty years has felt himself rushed on from one change to the next. That which yesterday was a mere utopian novel about the future, portraying unfulfillable dreams as though they were realities, today has been left behind by development and now appears as child's play beside that which we have experienced and a very modest aspiration beside that which begins to be possible. The dream of Daedalus and Icarus of flying in the heavens is no longer a myth that merely resigns itself to corroborating the earthbound solidity of man, for whom wings are unattainable, but, rather, has been fulfilled. The hand of man reaches out into the heavens; nothing is impossible any more. The sharply defined contours of being are becoming blurred; the mobility of all that is real becomes ever more obvious; the theory of evolution is becoming credible and practicable—through man's interior experience, as it were. At one time the world was characterized by continuity. Customs and aspirations were the same from generation to generation. Men and things seemed to be ruled by a fixed decree. Change in the fixed order was unthinkable, even if seen to be scientifically possible and

right. Today, we are witnesses of the indeterminateness of all that exists, witnesses of a reality
that consists, not in being, but in becoming.

The man of today looks toward the future. His
slogan is "Progress", not "Tradition"; "Hope",
not "Faith". He is moved, it is true, by a certain romanticism about the past. He delights in
surrounding himself with precious things of history, but all of this serves only to confirm that
these times are past and that the empire of the
man of today is tomorrow, the world he himself is going to build. For that to which he looks
forward is not, as in the early Church, the kingdom of God, but the kingdom of man, not the
return of the Son of Man, but the final victory of
a rational, free, and brotherly order among men
who have discovered themselves. The development through which we are living presents itself,
not as a gift from on high, but as the product
of hard work, of planned, calculated, and inventive activity. Thus, for the man of today hope no
longer means looking for things over which we
have no control, but action by our own power.
Man expects redemption to come from himself,
and he seems to be in a position to provide it. In

this way the primacy of the future is linked with the primacy of practice, the primacy of human activity above all other attitudes. Theology, too, is becoming more and more invaded by this attitude. "Orthopractice" takes the place of orthodoxy, and "eschatopractice" becomes more important than eschatology. If in former days it was left to popular enlightenment to tell the peasants that chemical fertilizers were more efficacious than prayer, now—a decent interval having elapsed—we can read the same sort of thing in modern "religious" literature that is straining to be "with it". There, too, we may find it argued that in certain circumstances prayer will have to be "remodeled": it can scarcely any longer be regarded as an invocation of divine assistance, but must be regarded as recollection serving the practice of self-help. Belief in progress—often said to be dead—is taking on a new lease of life, and the optimism that preaches that man will at last really be able to build the city of man is finding a fresh following.

The city of man, to many the symbol of all they desire, inspires in others only feelings of melancholy. For as hope arises, so does fear begin to spread. The anxiety that seemed to have been exorcized in the optimistic immediate post-war years once more awakes. When the first man set foot on the moon, no one was able to avoid feeling pride and joy and enthusiasm over man's colossal achievement. The event was felt, not as a victory over a nation, but as a victory for mankind. But this moment of joy had its mixture of sadness, for no one could escape the thought that this same man, who is capable of such marvelous things, is unable to prevent millions of men dying of hunger every year, has to allow millions to live without human dignity, is unable to put a stop to war or to stem the rising tide of crime. The road to the moon is easier to find than the road to man himself. Technical "know-how" is not necessarily human "know-how". Quite obviously knowledge of how to deal with himself lies on a totally different plane from technical accomplishment.

We want to follow this line of thought farther. Technology creates new opportunities for humanity. This cannot be disputed. A Christian has no grounds for any kind of resentment of technology. Anyone who grew up in the pre-technical age is unlikely to be tempted to fall for the romanticism of nature. He knows how hard things were in those days, how much inhumanity there could be in the nontechnical world; he knows just how many things have become better and more beautiful and more human now. But this same technical skill which offers such opportunities to humanity offers also fresh opportunities to the one who is anti-humane. There is no need to speak of the ultimate horrors of atomic weapons and of biological and chemical warfare, although the store of terror they imply always lurks somewhere in our minds. We need only take a look at the "city of man". Ever-increased planning means ever more regimentation of men. The eruptions that shatter our modern society are no doubt an unconscious rebellion against the complete planning of our existence, which creates a sense of suffocation, against which man wants to defend himself and finds that he cannot. Planning creates dependence and hence an impotence of the individual such as has never been known before. In addition we detect the ominous effects of our own activities: air, water, the earth—the very elements by which we live are threatened with destruction by the poisonous breath of our techniques; the energies upon which we depend seem, by their by-products, to be turning into the forces of our eventual annihilation. The city of man is beginning to strike terror into our hearts—it could become the tombstone of humanity.[3]

It would be far too simple to take out the sledgehammer of the theologian at this point and say: let us, then, be saved *from* technology, not *by* technology; let us find hope through faith and not against faith. Such a God would resemble all too closely the *deus ex machina* of Greek tragedy, who in Euripides had already become a joke at the expense of the gods and of faith. Euripides seems to be saying: The world is in such a state that only the sudden appearance of God can set it in order; but such a God exists only in our theaters. And so with Euripides, tragedy becomes more tragic than ever, for there is no way out, it seems, for reality remains without God and out of joint. The Christian God came, not as a *deus ex machina* to set everything externally in order, but as the Son of Man in order interiorly to share in the passion of mankind. And this, too, is pre-

---

[3] P. H. Simon carefully weighs up this ambivalence of the modern developments in chapter 3 of *Ce que je crois* (Paris: Grasset, 1966).

cisely the task of the Christian: to share in the passion of mankind from within, to extend the sphere of human being so that it will find room for the presence of God.

It is in this context that we must understand the striking optimism with which the Vatican Council viewed the technological age and judged its advances to be realizations of the primeval commission to man to subdue the whole earth.[4] To think thus is not, however, to acquiesce in the euphoria of an uncritical technical consciousness that has not yet become conscious of its own abysmal depths. On the contrary, it is to know that an emptied heaven will not suffice to create a blissful earth, as many of the prophets of the new humanity seem to think. Nor does it demand a flight into the romanticism of pure nature or the handing of man over to passivity. To create the city of man becomes a rational project when one knows who man is, when one has found the measure of his humanity. Then technology becomes hope, when it takes its direction from the

---

[4] Pastoral Constitution on the Church in the Modern World, pt. 1, chap. 3, esp. no. 34. Cf. the commentary by A. Auer in LThK, supplement 3, "Das Zweite Vatikanische Konzil" (Freiburg i. Br., 1968), pp. 377–97.

core of man's nature—the image of God in man. The affirmation of the Council that the Christian message neither hinders men from building up the world nor encourages the neglect of human welfare may sound a bit apologetic.[5] But when we take a comprehensive look at the factors operating in history, it proves to be illuminating and convincing. Man is the hope of mankind as he certainly is also the hell of mankind and a constant threat to mankind. That faith can well and truly place its hope in man is because, for faith, man is no longer an unpredictable being—as he is progressively coming to know himself—but in the end is Jesus Christ. In him, for the first time definitively, is man the hope of humanity. That means at the same time that God did not want to become the hope of mankind except by himself becoming man. The kingdom of God will be the city of man. The New Testament concludes with a vision of this city. It is true that this city spells the end of all our planning and its

---

[5] Pastoral Constitution on the Church in the Modern World, pt. 1, chap. 3, no. 34: "Hence it is clear that men are not deterred by the Christian message from building up the world or impelled to neglect the welfare of their fellows. They are, rather, more stringently bound to do these very things."

collapse. It comes down from above. But it only comes because and when man has run and suffered the whole course of his human existence to the limits of his capacities. And so in the meantime we are left simply with the task of corroborating the affirmation of faith that in Christ man has become the hope of humanity, by living our own lives in terms of this model, seeking to become one another's hope and to set upon the future the seal of Christ's features—the features of the coming city that will be completely human because it belongs completely to God.

What Will the Future Church Look Like?

The theologian is no soothsayer; nor is he a futurologist, who makes a calculation of the future based on the measurable factors of the present. His profession very largely withdraws from calculation. Only very slightly, therefore, might it become concerned with futurology, which itself is no soothsaying; rather, it ascertains what is calculable and has to leave the incalculable an open question. Because faith and the Church reach down into those depths from which creative newness, the unexpected and the unplanned, are constantly coming forth, their future remains hidden to us, even in an age of futurology. When Pius XII died, who could have foreseen the Second Vatican Council or the postconciliar development? Or who would have dared to foretell the First Vatican Council when Pius VI, abducted by the troops of the young French Republic, died a prisoner in Valence in 1799? Three years earlier one of the directors of the Republic had written: "This old idol will be destroyed. This is what freedom and philosophy desire. . . . It is to be hoped that Pius VI will live two years longer to give philosophy time to complete its work and leave this lama of Europe without a successor."[1] Things were in such a bad way that funeral orations were delivered on the papacy, which people were forced to regard as extinguished forever.

Let us, therefore, be cautious in our prognostications. What Saint Augustine said is still true: Man is an abyss; what will rise out of these depths, no one can see in advance. And whoever believes that the Church is not only determined by the abyss that is man, but reaches down into the greater, infinite abyss that is God will be the first to hesitate with his predictions, for this naive desire to know for sure could only be the announcement of his own historical

---

[1] Quoted by F. X. Seppelt and G. Schwaiger, *Geschichte der Päpste* (Munich, 1964), pp. 367f. Cf. also the exposition in L. J. Rogier and G. de Bertier de Sauvigny, *Geschichte der Kirche*, vol. 4 (Einsiedeln, 1966), pp. 177ff. Summing up, G. de Bertier de Sauvigny says of the situation at the end of the Enlightenment: "In short, if Christianity still had any chance of survival at the beginning of the nineteenth century, this lay more on the side of the Churches of the Reformed tradition than on the side of the Catholic Church, which had been stricken in head and members" (p. 181).

ineptitude. Does the title of this chapter have any meaning in that case? It has, provided we bear our limitations well in mind. It is precisely in times of vehement historical upheaval, when all the past seems to dissolve and completely new things seem to emerge, that men need to reflect upon history, which enables them to see the unreal exaggeration of the moment in the right perspective and integrates them again into a happening that never repeats itself but, on the other hand, never loses its unity and its context. You might say: "Have we heard correctly; reflection upon history? That means looking back into the past, and we were expecting a glimpse into the future." You have heard correctly; but I maintain that reflection upon history, properly understood, embraces both looking back into the past and, with that as the starting point, reflecting on the possibilities and tasks of the future, which can only become clear if we survey a fairly long stretch of the road and do not naively shut ourselves up in the present. Looking back into the past does not yield a prediction of the future, but it limits our illusion of complete uniqueness and shows us that while exactly the same did not happen before, something very similar did. The dissimilarity between then and now is the reason for the uncertainty of our statements and for the newness of our tasks; the similarity is the basis for orientation and correction.

The period in the past that bears the greatest resemblance to the present situation in the Church is, first, that of so-called Modernism about the turn of the century and, then, the end of the rococo period, which marked the decisive emergence of the modern period, with the Enlightenment and the French Revolution. The crisis of Modernism never really came to a head, but it was interrupted by the measure taken by Pius X and by the change in the intellectual situation after the First World War. The crisis of the present is but the long-deferred resumption of what began in those days. The analogy of the history of the Church and of theology in the period of the Enlightenment remains with us, therefore. Whoever looks more closely will be amazed at the extent of the similarity between then and now. Today the Enlightenment as a historical epoch does not enjoy a very high reputation; even those who resolutely follow the trail of the things of that period do not want to be known as the "Enlightened" but keep their distance from that category and gravitate to the simple rationalism of the period, insofar as they take the trouble to mention historical events at all. And here we find our first analogy in the resolute rejection of history, which is counted as no more than the storeroom of yesterday—of no use at all to the utterly new today. We find a triumphant certainty that it is no longer tradition but rationality that governs action; the key words are "rational", "intelligible", and so on. In all of these things, the Enlightenment is astonishingly like the present day. But perhaps even before mentioning these facts, which seem to me to be negative, one ought to take a look at the characteristic mixture of one-sidedness and positive beginnings that link the Enlightened of then and now and that cause the present to appear not so utterly new after all and not so exempt from all historical comparison.

The Enlightenment had its liturgical movement, the aim of which was to simplify the liturgy and restore it to its original basic structure. Excesses in the cult of relics and of saints were to be removed, and, above all, the vernacular, with congregational singing and participation, was to be introduced. The Enlightenment witnessed also an episcopal movement that

wanted to stress the importance of the bish-
ops over against the one-sided centralization of
Rome. This movement had democratic elements,
as when Wessenberg, the vicar general of Constance, demanded the setting up of provincial
synods. Reading his works, one imagines one is
reading a progressive of the year 1969. The abo-
lition of celibacy was demanded; the sacraments
were to be administered only in the vernacular;
and no promises were to be required concerning
the religious education of the children of a mixed
marriage, and so on. That Wessenberg wanted to
see regular preaching, a raising of the standard of
religious education, and encouragement of biblical studies proves once again that these men were
by no means moved merely by a reckless rationalism. Nonetheless, we are left with the impression of an ambivalent figure, because in the last
analysis, only the garden shears of constructive
reason are at work, capable of producing many
good things, but insufficient if they are the only
tool at our disposal.[2] We receive the same im-

---

[2] Cf. the instructive article on Wessenberg by Archbishop C.
Gröber in the first edition of LThK 10:835–39; LThK, 2nd ed.,
10:1064ff. (W. Müller). The publication of the works of Wessenberg has been taken in hand by K. Aland.

pression of ambivalence when we read the pro-
ceedings of the synod of Pistoia, a council at-
tended during the Enlightenment by 234 bish-
ops in 1786 in northern Italy. This synod tried to
translate the reforming ideas of that period into
realities in the Church, but it came to grief on
the mixture of genuine reform with naive rationalism. Once again one thinks that one is reading
a postconciliar book when one comes across the
assertion that a spiritual ministry is not directly
ordained by Christ but merely comes forth out of
the life of the Church, which itself is uniformly
priestly, or when one reads that a celebration of
the Mass without Holy Communion makes no
sense, or when the primacy of the papacy is described as purely functional, or, conversely, the
divine right of the episcopal office is stressed.[3]
It is true that a great many of the propositions
of Pistoia were condemned by Pius VI in 1794.
The one-sidedness of this synod had discredited
even its good ideas.

The most successful way to discover the embryo of the future in any particular epoch is to

---

[3] See the documentation in Denzinger-Schönmetzer, 2600–2700
esp. 2602, 2603, 2606, 2628. Cf. L. Willaert, "Synode von Pistoia",
in LThK, 2nd ed., 8:524f.

examine personalities and the signs of the times that they represent. Obviously, we can pick out only one or two characteristic personalities who embody the whole scope of the potential of that period and also manifest its astonishing analogy with the present. There were the extreme progressives, represented by, say, the melancholy figure of Gobel, the archbishop of Paris, who bravely went along with every step of progress in his own time. First he supported the idea of a constitutional national Church; then, when this was no longer enough, he abandoned his priesthood, declaring that since the happy outcome of the Revolution, no national religion was needed other than that of liberty and equality. He took part in the worship of the Goddess Reason in Notre Dame; but in the end, progress ran on ahead even of him. Under Robespierre, atheism was once again accounted a crime, and so the one-time bishop was led as an atheist to the guillotine and executed.[4]

In Germany the scene was quieter. We might mention Matthias Fingerlos, then the director of the Georgianum in Munich. In his book *What*

---

[4] Cf. Rogier, *Geschichte der Kirche*, 4:133ff.

Are Priests For? he explained that the priest ought primarily to be a teacher of the people, teaching them agriculture, animal husbandry, horticulture, the use of lightning conductors, and also music and art. Today we express this by saying that the priest ought to be a social worker, helping to build up an intelligent society, purified of all irrationalism.[5] Taking his place in the center —a moderate progressive, as it were—we would find Wessenberg, the vicar general of Constance, whom we have mentioned already and who certainly would not have agreed to the equation of faith with social work, but who, on the other hand, showed all too little liking for the organic, for the living thing, that fell outside the sheer constructions of reason. A totally different scale of values becomes evident when we encounter the somewhat later bishop of Regensburg, Johann Michael Sailer. It is difficult to place him. The current categories of progressive and conservative do not fit him, as the external course of his life proves. In 1794, he lost his professorship at Dillingen on a charge of supporting the

---

[5] A. Schmid, *Geschichte des Georgianums in München* (Regensburg, 1894), pp. 228ff.

Enlightenment; as late as 1819, his nomination to the bishopric of Augsburg was turned down as a result, among other things, of the opposition of Clemens Maria Hofbauer—later canonized— who saw Sailer still as a rationalist. On the other hand, in 1806, his pupil Zimmer was sent down from the university of Laudshut on a charge of being a reactionary. In Laudshut, Sailer and his circle were hated as opponents of the Enlightenment. The man whom Hofbauer regarded as a product of the Enlightenment was recognized by the true disciples of that movement as their most dangerous antagonist.[6]

They were right. This man and the wide circle of his friends and disciples started a movement that embodied far more of the future than did the triumphantly overbearing arrogance of the sheer

---

[6] On Sailer, cf. esp. I. Weilner, *Gottselige Innigkeit: Die Grundhaltung der religiösen Seele nach J. M. Sailer* (Regensburg, 1949); Weilner, "J. M. Sailer, Christliche Innerlichkeit", in *Grosse Gestalten christlicher Spiritualität*, ed. J. Sudbrack and J. Walsh, pp. 322–42. (Würzburg, 1969). On Zimmer, see the Tübingen dissertation by P. Schäfer, *Philosophie und Theologie im Übergang von der Aufklärung zur Romantik, dargestellt an P. B. Zimmer* (Philosophy and Theology in the Transition Period between the Enlightenment and the Romantic Age in P. B. Zimmer) [published in 1971 as vol. 3 of the Studien zur Theologie und Geistesgeschichte des neunzehnten Jahrhunderts, by Vandenhoeck and Ruprecht, Göttingen].

rationalists. Sailer was a man whose mind was open to all the problems of his time. The musty Jesuit scholasticism of Dillingen, into whose system reality could no longer be fitted, was bound to seem to him quite inadequate. Kant, Jacobi, Schelling, and Pestalozzi were his partners in dialogue. For him, faith was not tied to a system of propositions and could not be maintained by a flight into the irrational. It could survive only by entering into open discussion with the present. But this same Sailer had a profound grasp of the great theological and mystical tradition of the Middle Ages, uncommon in his time, because he did not confine man within the present moment but knew that if he is to become fully aware of himself, he must open his eyes reverently to the whole riches of his history. Above all, he was a man who not only thought but lived. If he was on the trail of a theology of the heart, that was not on account of cheap sentimentality but because he knew about the wholeness of man, who fulfills the unity of his being as the interpenetration of spirit and body, of the hidden springs of the mind and the clear vision of the intellect. Antoine de Saint-Exupéry once said: "One can

see properly only with the heart." If we com-
pare the lifeless progressivism of Matthias Fingerlos with the richness and depth of Sailer, the
truth of this saying becomes strikingly obvious.
Only with the heart can one see properly. Sailer
was a visionary because he had a heart. He was
able to give birth to something new, something
that was big with the future, because he lived by
what was enduring and because he placed himself, his whole life, at its disposal. This brings us
to the real point at last: only he who gives himself creates the future. The man who simply tries
to instruct, who wants to change *others*, remains
unfruitful.

And now we come to the other man, who was
an antagonist of both Sailer and of Wessenberg.
This was Clemens Maria Hofbauer, the Bohe-
mian baker's apprentice who became a saint.[7]
It is true that in many respects this man was
narrow-minded, even a bit of a reactionary; but
he was a man who loved, who placed himself at
the disposal of mankind with an unstinting and
unflagging passion. On the one hand, his cir-

---

[7] Cf. H. Gollowitzer, "Drei Bäckerjungen", *Catholica* 23 (1969):
147–53.

cle included men like Schlegel, Brentano, and Eichendorff; on the other hand, he unreservedly took up the cause of the poorest and most abandoned, seeking nothing for himself, ready to suffer any ignominy if thereby he could help someone. Thus men were able to rediscover God through him, just as he had discovered men through God and knew that they required more than instruction in agriculture and animal husbandry. In the end, the faith of this poor baker's apprentice proved to be more humane and more reasonable than the academic rationality of the mere Rationalists. And so the thing that outlived the ruins of the declining eighteenth century and was reborn as the future was something very different from that which Gobel or Fingerlos had suspected. It was a Church, reduced in size, diminished in social prestige, but a Church that had become fruitful from a new interior power, which released new formative and social forces, manifested both in great lay movements and in the founding of numerous religious congregations, all of which are very much part and parcel of the Church's most recent history.

We have arrived, then, at the present day and find ourselves looking toward tomorrow. Today, likewise, the future of the Church can and will issue from those whose roots are deep and who live from the pure fullness of their faith. It will not issue from those who accommodate themselves merely to the passing moment or from those who merely criticize others and assume that they themselves are infallible measuring rods; nor will it issue from those who take the easier road, who sidestep the passion of faith, declaring false and obsolete, tyrannous and legalistic, all that makes demands upon men, that hurts them and compels them to sacrifice themselves. To put this more positively: the future of the Church, once again as always, will be reshaped by saints, by men, that is, whose minds probe deeper than the slogans of the day, who see more than others see, because their lives embrace a wider reality. Unselfishness, which makes men free, is attained only through the patience of small daily acts of self-denial. By this daily passion, which alone reveals to a man in how many ways he is enslaved by his own ego, by this daily passion and by it alone, a man's eyes are slowly opened. He sees only to the extent that he has lived and suffered. If today we are scarcely able any longer to

become aware of God, that is because we find
it so easy to evade ourselves, to flee from the
depths of our being by means of the narcotic of
some pleasure or other. Thus our own interior
depths remain closed to us. If it is true that a
man can see only with his heart, then how blind
we all are![8]

How does all of this affect the problem we are
examining? It means that the big talk of those
who prophesy a Church without God and without faith is all empty chatter. We have no need
of a Church that celebrates the cult of action in
political prayers. It is utterly superfluous. Therefore, it will destroy itself. What will remain is the
Church of Jesus Christ, the Church that believes
in the God who has become man and promises
us life beyond death. The kind of priest who is
no more than a social worker can be replaced by
the psychotherapist and other specialists; but the
priest who is no specialist, who does not stand

---

[8] On this topic, cf. the magnificent exposition by H. de Lubac, "Ho-
liness in Future" in *The Church: Paradox and Mystery*, trans. James R.
Dunne (Alba House, 1969), pp. 122–27. Cf. De Lubac, "L'Église
dans la crise actuelle", *Nouvelle Revue théol.* 91 (1969): 580–96, esp.
pp. 592ff.

on the sidelines, watching the game, giving offi-
cial advice, but in the name of God places himself at the disposal of men, who is beside them in
their sorrows, in their joys, in their hope and in
their fear, such a priest will certainly be needed
in the future.

Let us go a step farther. From the crisis of
today the Church of tomorrow will emerge—
a Church that has lost much. She will become
small and will have to start afresh more or less
from the beginning. She will no longer be able
to inhabit many of the edifices she built in pros-
perity. As the number of her adherents diminishes, so will she lose many of her social privi-
leges. In contrast to an earlier age, she will be
seen much more as a voluntary society, entered
only by free decision. As a small society, she will
make much bigger demands on the initiative of
her individual members. Undoubtedly she will
discover new forms of ministry and will ordain to
the priesthood approved Christians who pursue
some profession. In many smaller congregations
or in self-contained social groups, pastoral care
will normally be provided in this fashion. Alongside this, the full-time ministry of the priesthood

will be indispensable as formerly. But in all of the changes at which one might guess, the Church will find her essence afresh and with full conviction in that which was always at her center: faith in the triune God, in Jesus Christ, the Son of God made man, in the presence of the Spirit until the end of the world. In faith and prayer she will again recognize her true center and experience the sacraments again as the worship of God and not as a subject for liturgical scholarship.

The Church will be a more spiritual Church, not presuming upon a political mandate, flirting as little with the Left as with the Right. It will be hard going for the Church, for the process of crystalization and clarification will cost her much valuable energy. It will make her poor and cause her to become the Church of the meek. The process will be all the more arduous, for sectarian narrow-mindedness as well as pompous self-will will have to be shed. One may predict that all of this will take time. The process will be long and wearisome as was the road from the false progressivism of the eve of the French Revolution—when a bishop might be thought smart if he made fun of dogmas and even insinuated that the existence of God was by no means certain[9] —to the renewal of the nineteenth century. But when the trial of this sifting is past, a great power will flow from a more spiritualized and simplified Church. Men in a totally planned world will find themselves unspeakably lonely. If they have completely lost sight of God, they will feel the whole horror of their poverty. Then they will discover the little flock of believers as something wholly new. They will discover it as a hope that is meant for them, an answer for which they have always been searching in secret.

And so it seems certain to me that the Church is facing very hard times. The real crisis has scarcely begun. We will have to count on terrific upheavals. But I am equally certain about what will remain at the end: not the Church of the political cult, which is dead already with Gobel, but the Church of faith. She may well no longer be the dominant social power to the extent that she was until recently; but she will enjoy a fresh blossoming and be seen as man's home, where he will find life and hope beyond death.

---

[9] Cf. Rogier, *Geschichte der Kirche*, 4:121.